HOCKEY
LEAGUES AND TOURNAMENTS

DAVID AND PATRICIA ARMENTROUT

The Rourke Press, Inc.
Vero Beach, Florida 32964

Patricia and David Armentrout specialize in nonfiction writing and have had several book series published for primary schools. They reside in Cincinnati with their two children.

PROJECT EDITORS:
Dick Doughty is a former Elementary School teacher who now operates his own business. He coached hockey for 9 years from the minor level through Junior "A." Dick is a certified Level 3 OMHA referee and is currently Referee-in-Chief for his hometown minor hockey association.

Rob Purdy has been a Secondary School teacher for 16 years. He is a certified Advance I hockey coach and a NCCP coaching instructor. Rob has coached hockey for 10 years in the OMHA, with a Pee Wee championship in 1997.

PHOTO CREDITS:
All photos © Kim Karpeles except © Frank Grant/Intl Stock: page 7; © Ian Tomlinson/Allsport: page 23; © Rick Stewart/Allsport: page 24; © Al Bello/Allsport: pages 26, 39, 40; © East Coast Studios: page 4

EDITORIAL SERVICES:
Penworthy Learning Systems

Library of Congress Cataloging-in-Publication Data

Armentrout, David, 1962-
    Hockey—leagues and tournaments / David Armentrout, Patricia Armentrout.
        p. cm. — (Hockey)
    Includes index.
    Summary: Discusses aspects of organized hockey, including its history, youth leagues, minor leagues, college hockey, women's leagues, the National Hockey League, the Olympics, and how to join a hockey league.
    ISBN 1-57103-220-7
    1. Hockey—Juvenile literature. 2. Hockey—Tournaments—Juvenile literature.
[1. Hockey—Tournaments.] I. Armentrout, Patricia, 1960-   . II. Title. III. Series:
Armentrout, David, 1962- Hockey.
QV847.25.A75 1998
796.962—dc21   98–28438
                                                                          CIP
                                                                          AC

Printed in the USA

TABLE OF CONTENTS

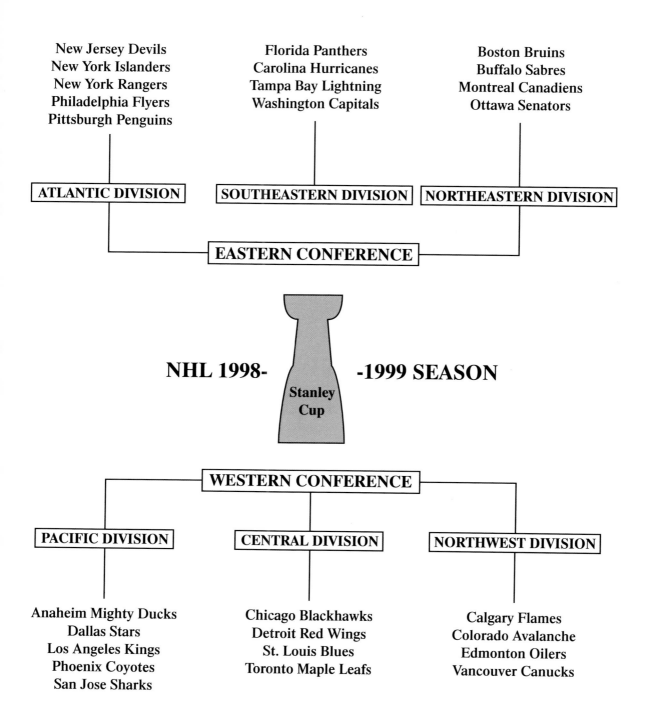

New Jersey Devils
New York Islanders
New York Rangers
Philadelphia Flyers
Pittsburgh Penguins

Florida Panthers
Carolina Hurricanes
Tampa Bay Lightning
Washington Capitals

Boston Bruins
Buffalo Sabres
Montreal Canadiens
Ottawa Senators

ATLANTIC DIVISION

SOUTHEASTERN DIVISION

NORTHEASTERN DIVISION

EASTERN CONFERENCE

NHL 1998- Stanley Cup -1999 SEASON

WESTERN CONFERENCE

PACIFIC DIVISION

CENTRAL DIVISION

NORTHWEST DIVISION

Anaheim Mighty Ducks
Dallas Stars
Los Angeles Kings
Phoenix Coyotes
San Jose Sharks

Chicago Blackhawks
Detroit Red Wings
St. Louis Blues
Toronto Maple Leafs

Calgary Flames
Colorado Avalanche
Edmonton Oilers
Vancouver Canucks

CHAPTER ONE

ICE HOCKEY HISTORY AND DEVELOPMENT

Indoor ice rinks make it possible to play ice hockey all year, in any climate, but it wasn't always that way. Ice hockey used to be only a northern sport—played outside—and only where the temperature stayed cold long enough to freeze the surface of ponds and lakes.

Today you can find indoor ice rinks in every state in the U.S. Thanks to indoor ice rinks, hockey is becoming popular all over the world. Even warm countries such as Mexico boast several hockey teams.

Hockey Beginnings

Ice hockey may have started in northern Europe, but no one knows for sure. Field hockey was a popular summer sport in Europe during the 15th century. Athletes who couldn't get enough of the game in the summer, began to use the frozen surface of ponds and lakes to play their game in the winter. The slippery ice added a new dimension to the sport.

North American ice hockey, as we know it, has its roots in Canada. The first ice hockey games may have been played by British soldiers stationed at a base in Halifax, Nova Scotia. Some historians also credit students at McGill University in Montreal with playing the first organized games at a downtown rink. Many of the rules were adopted from the Native American game of **lacrosse**, a field game played using a ball and a netted stick. Where and how ice hockey began is uncertain. There is no doubt that it has become an extremely popular, highly organized team sport.

★ DID YOU KNOW?

Ice hockey teams originally had nine players on the ice. Over the years the number of players dropped to the present six positions: Center, Right Forward (or Right Wing), Left Forward (or Left Wing), Right Defense, Left Defense, and Goalie.

Local residents enjoy a game on a frozen pond.

A 2-minute penalty can seem like a very long time.

League Development

Today, there are hockey leagues for children, teens, adults, and seniors. There are professional minor league teams and professional major league teams. A new league exists for disabled athletes. The professional teams receive a lot of attention due to the television broadcasts of their games. But amateur hockey is growing, as shown by the number of amateur leagues opening up across the United States.

Adult Leagues

Women's hockey dates back more than a century, but it did not become popular until the 1990s. Today, more than 60 colleges across the nation have women's hockey programs.

Professional women's hockey leagues have existed in Europe for some time. The first professional women's league in North America, the Women's Professional Hockey League (WPHL), was organized in 1998 and will open its first season with four teams.

Women's hockey made its Olympic debut in the 1998 winter games. Teams from six countries competed for the gold medal. The U.S. Women's team won the gold medal.

Men's adult leagues start with the junior leagues. Junior hockey not only offers players a chance to play the game but also provides male players an opportunity to improve their skills and work toward college hockey or a career in professional hockey.

Senior leagues are available for adult hockey players. The senior leagues have a division that permits **body-checking** and a division that does not permit it. Both divisions have leagues for players who are age 30 and over and age 35 and older (goalies can be 25 years of age). A player who has played on a college, junior college, or professional hockey team cannot play on a senior league team in that same hockey season.

Players take turns taking shots on goal.

A coach gives last-minute instructions before a game.

College Hockey

Interest in college hockey is on the rise. One reason is that many college players have moved on to play in the National Hockey League (NHL), giving college hockey more publicity. A second reason is that college hockey programs have improved over the years. Today there are over 100 men's college hockey teams across the United States. Ten years ago only a handful of colleges had a strong hockey program. Now at least 20 programs excel in ice hockey.

College hockey games are filling arenas these days because they are fun to watch. The college game is somewhat different from an NHL game. College hockey rules are not the same as NHL rules. For example, the center red line is removed to allow for two line passes, stretching the playing surface and displaying the speed and finesse of the players.

YOUTH HOCKEY

While professional ice hockey leagues get most of the attention, it is the amateur leagues—especially the youth leagues—that are the backbone of the sport. Every Saturday morning across the United States and Canada, children of all ages strap on their pads, lace up their boots, and skate onto the ice at their local rink. Children enjoy the sport whether they are good at it or not. They show their enthusiasm for the game as they drag their parents out of the house so they can get to their scheduled practices.

Organized youth leagues are all over North America. Most leagues begin in the fall and end in early spring. Some cities have spring and summer leagues that run through June. Still others run all year long.

Choosing the right league will depend on your playing style and interest. Some leagues are "competitive" while others are "recreational." **Competitive league** teams travel during their playing season, playing half of their games "on the road." **Recreational league** teams play against each other and usually share a local rink. Young children and players who are less experienced often play in recreational leagues. Older players who have had the opportunity to work on their skating and game skills are more often seen playing in the competitive leagues.

If you are interested in joining a local youth league there are many ways to find leagues in your area. One way is to call your local hockey rink. You will either talk with someone on the phone who will answer your questions or hear a message about the league, what is required, and how and when you can register.

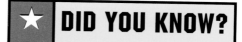

DID YOU KNOW?

USA Hockey has had an in-line hockey program since December of 1994. USA Hockey InLine provides support for the growth of the sport through a variety of educational programs. Membership packages include a subscription to *USA Hockey InLine Magazine.*

Ice time is expensive, and may have to be shared with another team.

Every hockey player must have good skating skills.

USA Hockey

USA Hockey, Inc., is the governing body of ice hockey in the United States. It is the American organization that can get you started in hockey even if you don't know how to skate. USA Hockey, based in Colorado Springs, Colorado, runs hockey programs all over the country. USA Hockey conducts tournaments, sponsors training and development camps, prints rule books and training manuals, and even publishes *American Hockey Magazine.* Members of USA Hockey receive the magazine free. USA Hockey membership also offers insurance benefits.

Below is a list of USA Hockey's age classifications for youth players.

For boys' teams
Midget—17 or under
Bantam—14 or under
Pee Wee—12 or under
Squirt—10 or under
Mite—8 or under
Mini-Mite—6 or under

For girls' teams
Midget—19 or under
Pee Wee—15 or under
Squirt—12 or under

DID YOU KNOW?

Did you know that the National Hockey League gets more players from the Canadian minor league system than from any other source?

USA Hockey keeps players and their parents in mind at all times. The organization works to provide the best hockey experience for both the parent and player while encouraging development in the sport. USA Hockey suggests game times for all age groups. The older players take later time slots for night games. For practices, they take the earliest morning hours. The youngest, least experienced players can use the rink in the middle of the day. USA Hockey also provides parents with a copy of the game rules and tips on buying the proper hockey equipment.

Ice hockey is a fast-paced team sport.

A professional hockey player demonstrates the slap shot at a roller hockey summer camp.

Canadian Youth Hockey

The Canadian Hockey Association links hockey players, parents, coaches, and officials with the most current hockey information. The association represents all of Canada and covers all levels of ice hockey.

The Canadian Hockey Association is the perfect source of information on youth leagues. It can advise parents on which type of league is best for their young player. It also has a program that teaches beginner hockey players everything from the **fundamental skills** of the game (like skating) to passing and shooting techniques. Fair play, fitness, and safety are stressed and trained parents are often the instructors.

The Canadian Hockey Association can also recommend hockey schools and camps. Hockey camps usually start in the summer for both girls and boys, and are often instructed by certified coaches and experienced players.

CHAPTER THREE

NATIONAL HOCKEY LEAGUE

The National Hockey League (NHL) is the largest professional hockey organization in the world. Professional hockey players are paid to play.

NHL History

Before World War I there were three professional hockey leagues: the International Pro Hockey League (which lasted about three years), the National Hockey Association (NHA), and the Pacific Coast League (PCL).

In 1914 the NHA and the PCL faced off in a game fighting for the Stanley Cup. When World War I broke out, the NHA ended.

After the war, in November of 1917, the National Hockey League was founded. The league's first games were played in December of that same year against teams in the Pacific Coast League.

The original five NHL teams were the Montreal Wanderers, the Quebec Bulldogs, the Toronto Arenas, the Montreal Canadiens, and the Ottawa Senators. The Quebec Bulldogs, however, decided not to play that first season and its players were sent to play for the other four teams.

The NHL's Toronto Arenas played the PCL's Vancouver Millionaires in 1918 and won the **Stanley Cup**. After the PCL ended, the NHL split into two divisions and took ownership of the Stanley Cup.

The Stanley Cup—probably the most famous trophy in sports—is the NHL's grand prize. The trophy was donated to the sport in 1893 by Lord Stanley of Preston, who served as the governor-general of Canada. The Stanley Cup is a silver bowl on top of a silver pedestal, or barrel. The names of the players and coaches from the best teams in hockey history are engraved on its sides.

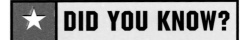 **DID YOU KNOW?**

Modern professional hockey rinks have changed a lot since 1917. New ice rinks are inside huge arenas built to hold thousands of fans comfortably. Most new arenas have the best sound and light systems around, restaurants, and private luxury boxes.

Wayne Gretzky started skating at age 3.

The Stanley Cup may be the most famous trophy in sports.

The 1998-1999 season of the National Hockey League, opens with 27 teams, or **franchises**. There are plans to expand the NHL to 30 teams by the year 2000. The NHL teams are based all over Canada and the United States.

The popularity of the NHL has never been greater. The NHL's championship series is now broadcast to no fewer than 140 countries around the world. Hundreds of millions of people, from North America to Africa, watch the final season games on television. The NHL has become more than just a game, it has become big business.

NHL Players

Currently there are more than 600 players in the NHL and that number will grow with the expansion of the league. Where do the players come from? Almost all professional players were developed in Canada in the past, but today star hockey players come from all over the world.

Canadians still account for over half of all NHL players, but athletes from at least 16 other countries played in the NHL in 1998. As the popularity of ice hockey continues to grow, the list of countries will grow, too.

DID YOU KNOW?

The NHL has grown fast since its humble beginnings, but the salaries of the players have grown even faster. A player earned an average pay of under $2,000 a year in the early days of the NHL. Today, the average salary has grown to over $1,000,000 a year.

NHL hockey players are bigger, faster, and stronger than ever before. The average player today stands over 6 feet (2 meters) tall and weighs 220 pounds (almost 100 kilograms)—14 pounds (over 6 kilograms) heavier than the players 20 years ago. This kind of growth is most likely the result of off-season conditioning programs that most players participate in. Whatever the reason, the highly skilled players of today are exciting to watch.

Division of the Teams

The NHL is divided into two conferences: the Eastern and the Western. At the start of the 1998-1999 season each conference had three divisions.

Professional hockey is exciting to watch.

Thick plexiglass protects the players and fans.

The Northeast, Southeast, and Atlantic divisions belong to the Eastern Conference. The Midwest, Central, and Pacific divisions belong to the Western Conference. Each division carried four or five teams. By the 2000-2001 season, each division will have five teams due to league expansion.

The Playoffs

Which teams go to the playoffs? Here is how it works: Each team earns points in the regular season based on its record. Two points are awarded for a win and one point is awarded for a tie. No points are earned for a loss. The teams with the best records play in conference games called "playoffs."

Each conference stages three playoff rounds, beginning with the conference quarterfinals and ending with the conference finals. The winners of the Eastern and Western Conference finals battle it out for the Stanley Cup Championship. The winner keeps the trophy for one year, when the process begins again.

MINOR LEAGUES

Minor league hockey is professional hockey—the players are paid to play the game. Minor leaguers generally play at a lower skill level than NHL players, and they don't earn salaries as high as the NHL players'.

Minor league hockey has grown in popularity. Just ten years ago there were only two minor leagues in the United States and now there are seven. The number of franchises, or teams, in the minors is constantly changing. Leagues add new teams every year.

Here is a list of the United States minor leagues in 1998:

the American Hockey League **AHL**
the International Hockey League **IHL**
the East Coast Hockey League **ECHL**
the Central Hockey League **CHL**
the United Hockey League **UHL**
the West Coast Hockey League **WCHL**
the Western Professional Hockey League **WPHL**

Some of the minor leagues have as few as 6 teams and others as many as 25 teams. With the growing interest in hockey today, we will surely see the number of minor leagues expand as well as the number of franchises in the leagues.

Minor League Skills

The minor leagues employ younger players who are still developing their hockey skills. Some players perform very well and break into the majors (NHL teams). Other players continue to play at a lower skill level, not quite up to NHL standards. But to the fans who enter the not-so-lavish arenas, the minor league teams can be just as exciting to watch as any NHL team.

★ DID YOU KNOW?

One difference between the minor leagues and the NHL is the number of games played per season. Generally, the minors play fewer games. The minor teams with the lowest skill level play the least number of games. For example, the NHL currently plays 82 games a season and the lowest-level minor league plays about 50.

Fans watch the action of a minor league game

A face-off occurs many times in a game.

The skill levels in the minors vary from player to player, and also from league to league The American and International Leagues (the two oldest minor leagues in the U.S.) have a high quality of play and are considered just one step below the NHL. The East Coast, United, and Central leagues are considered two or three steps down from the NHL. The West Coast and the Western Professional leagues are said to employ the youngest and least experienced players in professional hockey.

NHL Affiliates

The minors are considered the training grounds for hockey's major league, the NHL. Most minor league players hope to land a job with the NHL someday.

NHL franchises often have a working agreement with one or more minor league teams. The minor team is said to be an **affiliate** of the NHL team. As an example, the Charlotte Checkers (ECHL), and the Hartford Wolf Pack (AHL) are both affiliates of the NHL's New York Rangers. Sometimes players in the minors fill in gaps in the NHL line-up. This happens when the NHL team is low on players because of injuries.

Canadian Juniors

Canada has three minor leagues governed by the Canadian Hockey League. The leagues, known as "major junior leagues," are the Ontario Hockey League, Western Hockey League, and the Quebec Major Junior Hockey League.

Junior leaguers are between 16 and 20 years of age. They are selected from open tryouts or drafted from other teams. Although Canadian minor leagues are considered amateurs, the players do receive a small salary.

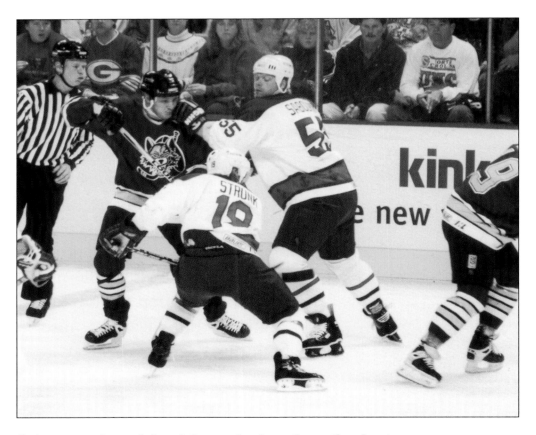

It is easy to lose sight of the puck when the action heats up.

Hockey is a game of concentration.

The players go to school in the cities where they play, and the money they are paid is more or less their living expenses.

The three junior leagues play by NHL rules with some differences. They get plenty of NHL scout exposure, and often provide the NHL with players. As a matter of fact, the players in the Canadian Hockey League are considered the future stars of the NHL.

The three leagues battle it out at the end of their season for the **Memorial Cup**—the Canadian Hockey League's version of the Stanley Cup.

OLYMPIC HOCKEY

For many athletes, there is no greater honor than to represent one's country in the **Olympic Games**. Olympic athletes are among the best in the world. Olympic athletes are considered amateurs. However, for the first time in Olympic history, professional players from the National Hockey League (NHL) were allowed to step down from their professional status and compete for their home countries at the 1998 Winter Olympics in Nagano, Japan.

Olympic Hockey History

Ice hockey was an Olympic event in 1920, when both winter and summer events were held at the same game. Ice hockey became a Winter Olympics event at the first winter games in 1924.

At the 1924 games in Chamonix, France, the Canadian team took the first Olympic medal in hockey. That team scored an incredible 110 goals in five games compared to only 3 goals scored by their opponents in the five games played. Canada continued to dominate ice hockey events by winning the gold medal in the next two Olympic competitions. Over time, other countries became more competitive as ice hockey grew more popular.

Women's Games

The United States women's Olympic hockey program is off to a great start. The U.S. team took the gold medal in 1998, at the first women's Olympic hockey competition. Six countries sent teams to the games in Nagano, Japan. The public greatly enjoyed the event. As a result, more women's teams will likely compete in the 2002 Winter Olympics.

★ DID YOU KNOW?

Women's equipment and protective gear are different from men's. Women's shoulder pads and pants are designed to fit the female form; and women wear a jill strap, or pelvic protector, compared to the jock strap of the men.

Winning the gold medal makes all the hard work worthwhile.

The best hockey players in the world compete in the Olympic Games.

Women's Olympic hockey is similar to men's hockey. Women's teams have 20 players on the roster and men's teams have 23. Both the men's and women's teams are allowed six players on the ice at any one time. Body-checking, common in men's games, is not allowed in women's ice hockey. This means women are able to focus more on their passing, stickhandling, and skating skills. The protective gear worn by women is specially designed to fit the female form and style of play.

Men's Games

Men's hockey has traditionally been one of the most popular Winter Olympic events. It is basically the same game played in the NHL. One difference between NHL and Olympic hockey is the size of the rink. The Olympic rink is 100 feet (about 30 1/2 meters) wide. The NHL rink is 85 feet (about 26 meters) wide on average. Both are 200 feet (about 61 meters) long.

The wider rink in Olympic hockey allows for a more open game, which means less congestion on the ice, especially behind the goals. This, in turn, reduces the amount of checking and other body contact between players, and places more importance on skating skills and speed.

★ DID YOU KNOW?

To equalize team abilities, sled hockey players are assigned points according to the severity of their disability. For example, players with good sitting balance and only slight limb impairment are given 3 points, while players with no sitting balance and major limb impairments are assigned 1 point. In most competitions, a team does not exceed 14 points.

Paralympic Hockey

Being disabled does not mean a person cannot compete in sports. In fact, disabled athletes from around the world are starting sports leagues in everything from basketball to—yes, you guessed it—ice hockey. Sledge, or sled, hockey is a **Paralympic** sport. The Paralympic Games are international events just like the Olympics, except the Paralympics are for disabled athletes.

Sled hockey is governed by many of the same rules used in regular hockey, but there are some obvious differences in the game. Sled hockey players sit on specially designed, lightweight sleds. The sleds are made of stainless steel or aluminum and have backrests for support.

Sled hockey rules are similar to traditional ice hockey rules.

Sled hockey players move along the ice by digging the metal picks of the sticks into the ice.

The sleds weigh between 12 and 18 pounds (5 1/2 and 8 kilograms). Ice hockey blades are attached under the sled. All sleds sit 3 1/2 inches (almost 9 centimeters) above the ice. This standard ensures that only sleds make contact during a game, not players.

Sled hockey players carry two sticks, or "picks." A sled hockey stick is shorter than a regular hockey stick. The top end of a stick, called the pick end, has a row of metal teeth. Players push themselves along the ice with the pick ends. Many players move at amazing speeds! The blade of the stick, like in traditional hockey, is used to shoot or pass the puck.

Sled hockey players are strapped to their sleds and wear protective equipment like the standard ice hockey equipment. The players change direction by shifting their body weight from side to side.

Sled hockey made its first appearance at the Paralympics in 1994, with teams from six countries competing. Its popularity at the 1998 games in Nagano, Japan, ensures that it will be a Paralympic event in the years to come.

GLOSSARY

affiliate (uh FIL ee it) — a minor league team that is partner of a major league (NHL) team

amateurs (AM uh terz) — people who play a sport without pay

body-checking (BAHD ee CHEK ing) — using the hips or shoulders to throw off an opponent who is in possession of the puck

competitive league (kum PET i tiv LEEG) — hockey league with teams that travel from city to city to compete

franchises (FRAN CHYZ ez) — professional sports teams

fundamental skills (fun deh MEN tl SKILZ) — basic skills like skating and stickhandling

lacrosse (luh KRAWS) — field game played by two opposing teams using a ball and a netted stick called a "crosse"

Memorial Cup (muh MOR ee ul KUP) — trophy awarded each year to the best team in the Canadian Hockey League

Olympic Games (o LIM pik GAYMZ) — international athletic contests for mostly amateur athletes

Paralympic Games (PAR uh LIM pik GAYMZ) — international athletic contests for disabled athletes

professional (pruh FESH uh nul) — someone paid to participate in a sport; a team made up of such players

GLOSSARY

recreational league (REK ree A shun nul LEEG) — hockey
league that consists of teams that compete against each
other and often share a local rink

sled hockey (SLED HOCK ee) — Paralympic sport and
form of ice hockey played by disabled players on sleds with
ice skate blades as runners

Stanley Cup (STAN lee KUP) — a trophy awarded each year
to the best team in the National Hockey League

FURTHER READING

Find out more with these helpful books and information sites:

Davidson, John, with John Steinbreder. *Hockey for Dummies An Official Publication of the NHL.* Foster City, CA: IDG Books Worldwide, Inc., 1997.

USA Hockey. *Official Rules of Ice Hockey.* Chicago:Triumph Books, 1997.

Official Rule Book of the Canadian Hockey Association. Canadian Hockey Association, 1997.

National Hockey League, The, and others. *The Official National Hockey League 75th Anniversary Commemorative Book. Toronto:* The Canadian Publishers, 1991.

Amateur Hockey Online Ice Hockey Rules at www.ll.net/aho/ah-rules.htm

American Sled Hockey Associationat www.SledHockey.org/

Canadian Hockey Association at www.canadianhockey.ca/

International Ice Hockey Federation (IIHF) at www.iihf.com

National Hockey League at www.nhl.com

USA Hockey, Inc. at www.usahockey.com

INDEX